WE HAVE A POPE

EMMAUS ROAD
PUBLISHING

Steubenville, Ohio
www.emmausroad.org

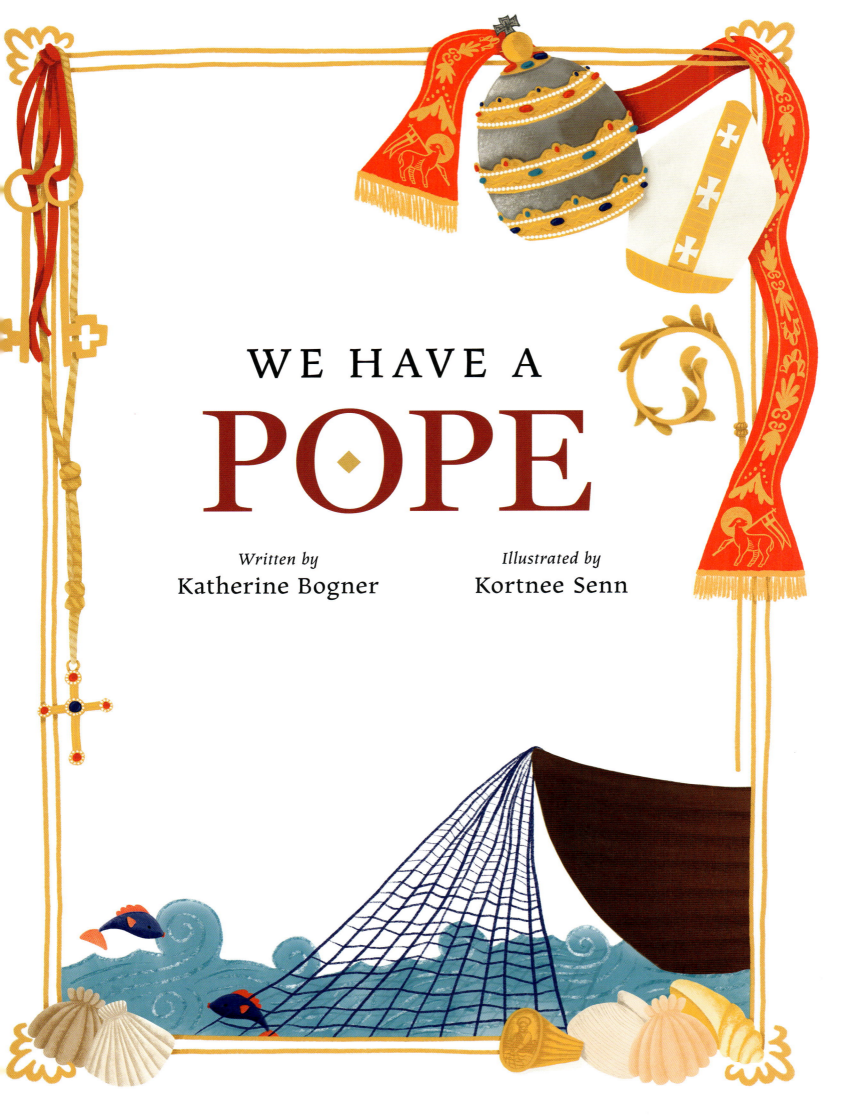

WE HAVE A POPE

Written by
Katherine Bogner

Illustrated by
Kortnee Senn

Emmaus Road Publishing
1468 Parkview Circle
Steubenville, Ohio 43952

©2024 Katherine Bogner & Kortnee Senn
All rights reserved. Published 2024
Printed in the United States of America
First Printing

Library of Congress Control Number:
ISBNs: 978-1-64585-363-3 Hardcover | 978-1-64585-364-0 Paperback |
978-1-64585-365-7 Ebook
Cover design and layout by Allison Merrick

Nihil obstat:
Msgr. Philip D. Halfacre, V.G.
Censor Librorum
Imprimatur:
Most Rev. Louis Tylka
Bishop of Peoria

October 23, 2023

The *nihil obstat* and *imprimatur* are declarations that a book or pamphlet is free of doctrinal or moral error. There is no implication that those who have granted the *nihil obstat* or *imprimatur* agree with the contents, opinions, or statements expressed therein.

To my littlest nephew, Owen Peter: May St. Peter guard, protect, and always guide
you to boldly declare your faith in Jesus Christ and the Church He established.
Love, Aunt Katie

For my husband, leader of our domestic church.
With love, Kortnee

*"And I tell you, you are Peter, and on this rock I will build my Church,
and the gates of Hades shall not prevail against it.
I will give you the keys of the kingdom of heaven,
and whatever you bind on earth shall be bound in heaven,
and whatever you loose on earth shall be loosed in heaven."*

MATTHEW 16:18–19

F rom the east and the west, the north and the south, cardinals from every corner of the world are gathering together in Rome, in the heart of the Catholic Church.

They've come to listen and to pray.

They've come to choose a new leader for Catholics everywhere.

It's time to elect a pope!

Who is the pope? He is . . .

    the Bishop of Rome,

    the Vicar of Christ,

    the Supreme Pontiff,

    the Servant of the Servants of God,

    and our Holy Father.

He guards, governs, and guides the whole Church as a good shepherd.

The pope carries on the mission of Jesus, uniting the one, holy, catholic, and apostolic Church.

Over two thousand years ago, Jesus made His Apostle Peter the very first pope. He named Peter the rock on which the Church would be built.

He called Peter to be a fisher of men who would lead God's people with unfailing faith. And not only that, Jesus gave Peter the keys to His Kingdom.

Those keys have been handed down from

Peter to each of his successors

in an unbroken line, right up to today.

All kingdoms of the world will come and go,

but the Kingdom of God will remain forever.

Who holds St. Peter's keys now?

When the successor to St. Peter dies, cardinals come together at the Vatican for a papal conclave to choose the new head of the Church on earth.

The conclave might take three days or three years. The cardinals will stay together until the Holy Spirit makes it clear whom God has chosen to lead his people.

Dressed all in red, the cardinal electors begin the conclave with Mass in St. Peter's Basilica and then process to the magnificent Sistine Chapel.

They sing the Litany of Saints, asking for the prayers of all the holy men and women in heaven.

They chant *Veni, Sancte Spiritus*—Come, Holy Spirit— calling for divine inspiration.

Above their heads, Michelangelo's paintings show God's mighty plan for creation and salvation.

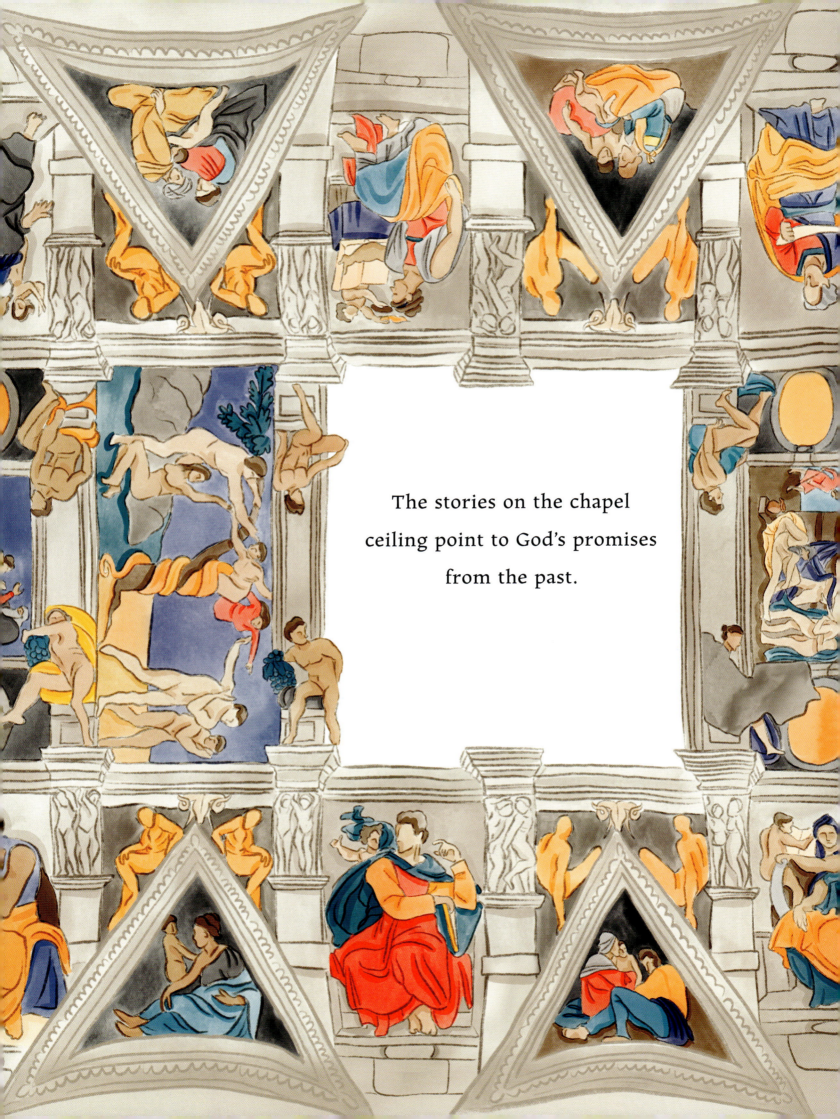

The stories on the chapel ceiling point to God's promises from the past.

Down below, the cardinals look to the future with hope. They pray to find a pontiff holy and humble, brave and bold. They ask God to send a pope who will be ready to share the story of God's plan with the whole world.

Locked inside with doors sealed tight, they are ready to hear the will of God. They close themselves in to keep out the distractions of the world. No letters, calls, or messages will take the cardinals from their task. Together they will wait until a decision is made.

Outside, the people of God gather to watch and pray. The arms of Bernini's colonnade open wide to welcome them to St. Peter's Square as they wait for the wind of the Holy Spirit to come and renew the Church.

In many languages, the people ask each other, "Is there any news?" The new pope could be from anywhere on the globe:

¿Hay noticias? Καθόλου νέα? Jakieś wieści?

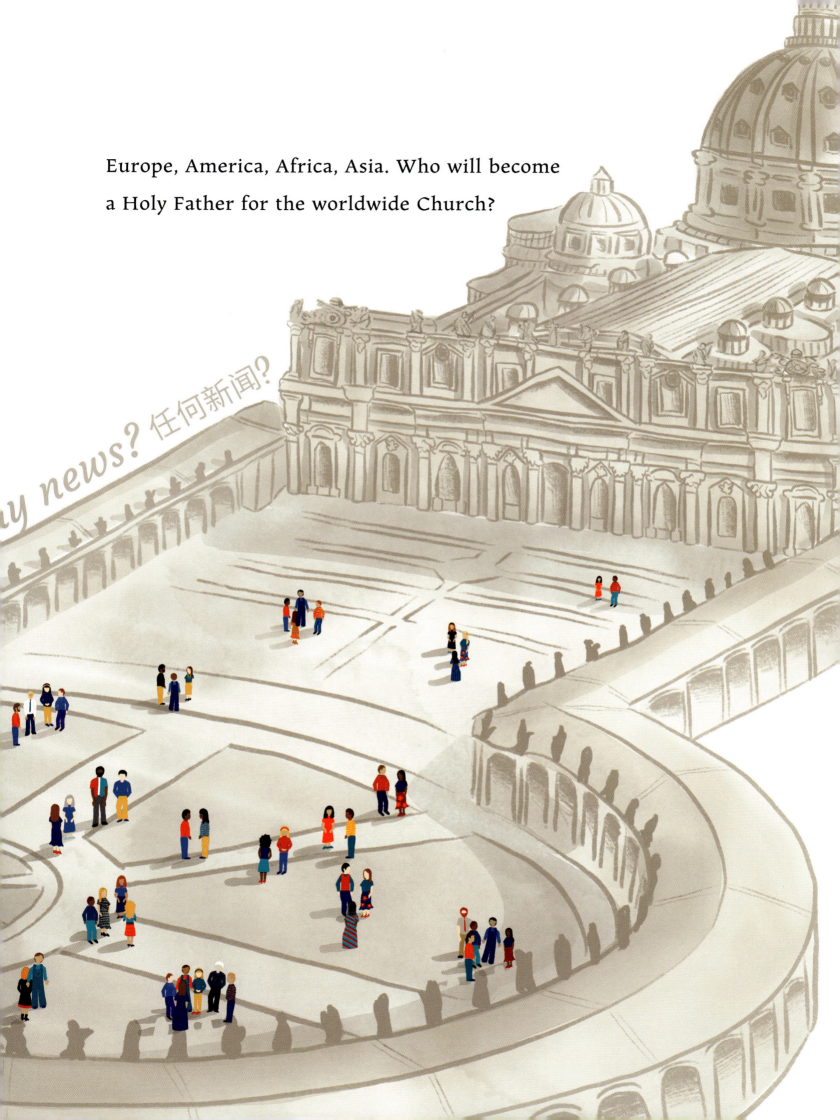

Europe, America, Africa, Asia. Who will become a Holy Father for the worldwide Church?

The cardinal electors begin their voting with a promise.

With his hand on the Gospel, each cardinal makes an oath to fulfill his duties faithfully.

Then, they each receive a secret ballot. The voting, or Scrutiny, has begun.

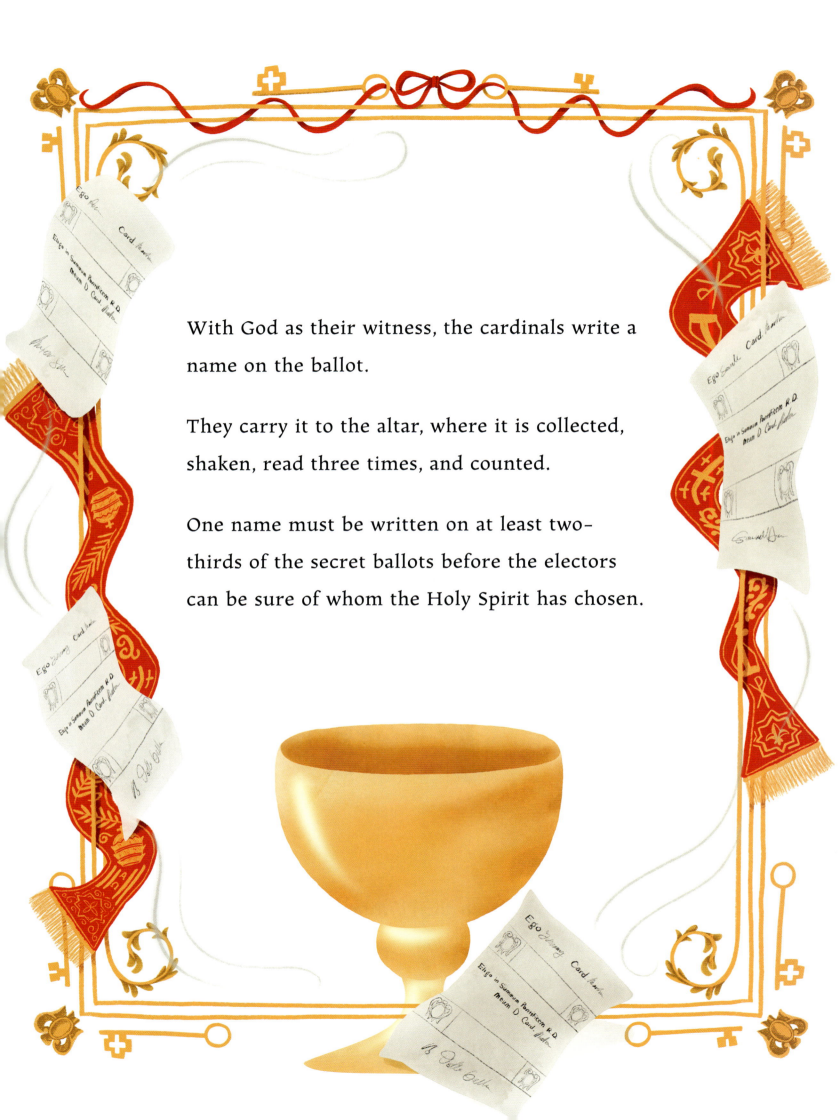

With God as their witness, the cardinals write a name on the ballot.

They carry it to the altar, where it is collected, shaken, read three times, and counted.

One name must be written on at least two-thirds of the secret ballots before the electors can be sure of whom the Holy Spirit has chosen.

At the end of each Scrutiny, the ballots are burned, sending streams of smoke through a special chimney in the roof of the Sistine Chapel.

When the smoke from the chimney rises black, the people know that more time is needed to choose the next pope. The cardinals must vote again.

Voting twice in the morning and twice in the afternoon, they continue waiting and praying until the answer is clear. Who will the new pope be?

When the ballots are counted and one name is written more than any other, the chosen man is called forward.

"Do you accept?"

If he answers yes, he must then choose the name by which he will be called.

With a new name, a new era begins. This pope will follow in the footsteps of St. Peter, guarding the keys of the Kingdom as he bears witness to Christ the King.

Now when the ballots are burned,

glorious white smoke billows

from the chapel chimney.

At the sight of it, the crowd swells and bells ring!

Inside the Room of Tears, the new pope pauses to reflect and pray as he dons his papal vestments for the first time. Dressed all in white, he is ready to meet his people.

"Papa! Papa!" the people cry as they wait to glimpse their new Holy Father. Who has been chosen?

The man in white steps out on the Benediction loggia to greet those below with great love. A brass band plays the Pontifical Anthem, and the smiling pope shares a blessing from Rome that reaches to the ends of the earth.

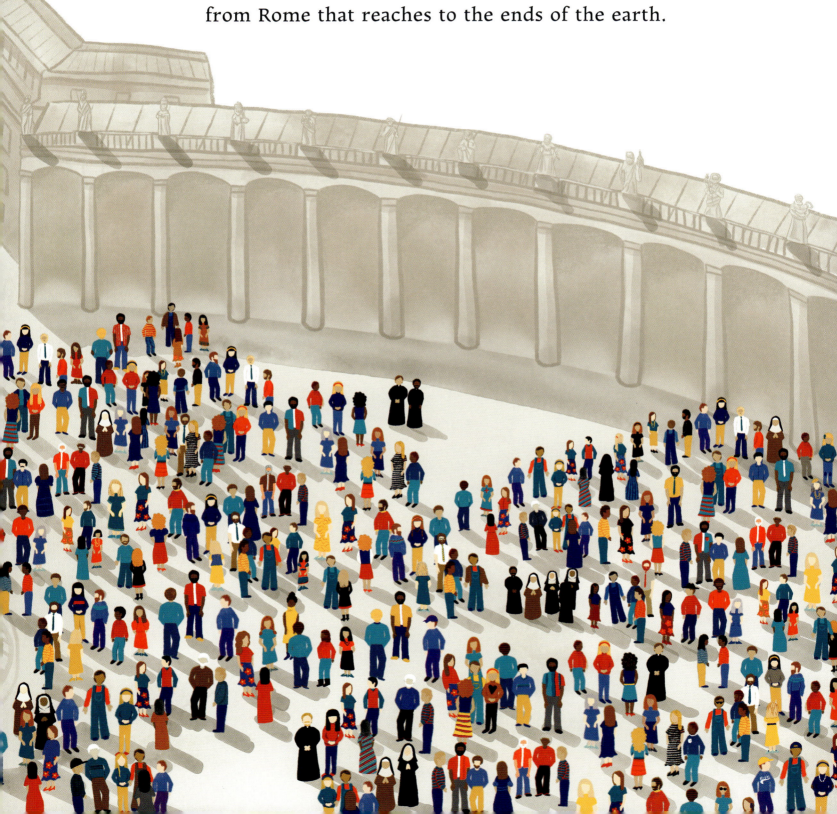

Around the world the good news resounds. Now from the east and the west, the north and the south, in every corner of the globe, the people of God rejoice as they hear:

HABEMUS PAPAM! WE HAVE A POPE!

Prayer for the Pope

In the name of the Father, and of the Son,
and of the Holy Spirit. Amen.

Dear Jesus,

Please bless our Holy Father, the pope.

Lead him to be a pontiff who is holy and humble,
brave and bold.

Help him follow in the footsteps of St. Peter
to guard the keys of the kingdom of heaven.

Make him a good shepherd who governs and guides
the whole Church.

May the pope serve You faithfully every day of his life.

Amen.

In the name of the Father, and of the Son,
and of the Holy Spirit. Amen.

Glossary

Apostolic: following the teaching of the Apostles; the bishops are the successors of the Apostles

Benediction loggia: balcony overlooking St. Peter's square used for the announcement of the new pope and the Urbi et Orbi blessing

Bernini's colonnade: hundreds of columns encircling St. Peter's Square, designed by Gian Lorenzo Bernini in the 1600s

Cardinal: a title bestowed by the pope, usually to a bishop; cardinals act as advisors to the pope and elect his successor

Cardinal elector: cardinal who is eligible to vote in a papal conclave

Catholic: means "universal"; the Catholic Church is for all people

Christ the King: title of Jesus; He is the eternal ruler of heaven and earth

Keys of St. Peter: not an actual set of keys; a symbol of the pope's authority to open and close the kingdom of heaven

Kingdom of God, or Kingdom of Heaven: not a place, but the truth that God reigns over all things including our hearts

Litany of Saints: prayer asking for the intercession of the saints, listing them by name

Michelangelo: artist from Italy who painted the murals on the walls and ceiling in the Sistine Chapel in the 1500s

One, holy, catholic, apostolic: the four marks of the Church

Papal conclave: gathering of cardinals at the Vatican after the death of a pope to vote for his successor

Papal vestments: special clothing worn by the pope

Pontifical Anthem: song played for special occasions, like announcing the entrance of the pope

Pope: leader of the Catholic Church on earth; titles include Holy Father, Bishop of Rome, Vicar of Christ, Supreme Pontiff, and Servant of the Servants of God

Rome: capital city of Italy, location of the Vatican city-state

Room of Tears: room just outside the Sistine Chapel where a newly elected pope dresses in his papal vestments before greeting the world; called the Room of Tears because it is a quiet place where the new pope has the chance to think and pray about the important responsibility God is asking of him

Scrutiny: the voting phase during a papal conclave

Sistine Chapel: chapel in the Vatican palace; location of papal conclaves

St. Peter's Basilica: papal basilica within the Vatican; built on the tomb of St. Peter

St. Peter's Square: the open space for gathering in front of St. Peter's Basilica

Successor: one who comes next in a line of leaders

Vatican: geographic center of the Catholic Church; independent city-state that is the smallest country in the world

Come, Holy Spirit

We believe that the election of a new pope is guided by the Holy Spirit. One common symbol of the Holy Spirit is a dove. Can you find all twelve of the Holy Spirit doves in the illustrations of this book?

Papal Succession

In the more than two thousand years since Jesus asked Peter to lead His Church on earth, there have been over 260 popes. One illustration in this book models the continuous leadership symbolically handing on the keys of St. Peter. The popes featured in that illustration are:

- St. Peter (r. 32–67)
- Pope St. Gregory the Great (r. 590–604)
- Pope St. Celestine V (r. 1294)
- Pope St. Pius V (r. 1566–1572)
- Pope Leo XIII (r. 1878–1903)
- Pope St. John Paul II (r. 1978–2005)

"Any News?"

During a conclave, people around the world wait to hear the news about the election of the new pope. Some people even travel to Rome to be present for the historic event. On one page in this book, a crowd starts to gather in St. Peter's Square, asking, "Is there any news?" The languages written above the colonnade include Spanish, Greek, Polish, English, and Mandarin.

Latin Phrases
USED DURING A CONCLAVE

Veni, Sancte Spiritus	Come, Holy Spirit
Eligo in Summum Pontificem	I elect as the Most High Pontiff
Acceptasne electionem de te canonice factam in Summum Pontificem?	Do you accept your canonical election as Supreme Pontiff?
Quo nomine vis vocari?	By what name do you wish to be called?
Urbi et Orbi	A blessing to the city (of Rome) and to the world
Habemus Papam!	We have a pope!

The Pope in the Bible

Want to read more about St. Peter and the role of the pope in Scripture? Here are a few places to start:

Matthew 4:18–20	Jesus calls Peter to become a fisher of men.
Matthew 16:15–19	Jesus gives Peter the keys to the Kingdom.
Luke 22:31–32	Jesus prays for Peter's faith so he can strengthen others.
John 10:14–16	Jesus says His flock will be cared for by one shepherd.
John 21:15–19	Jesus asks Peter to feed His sheep.
Acts 2:14–43	Peter leads the Early Church after Pentecost.